White Brown

poems by

Kayla Pica Williams

Finishing Line Press
Georgetown, Kentucky

White Brown

ACKNOWLEDGMENTS

"Online Dating" *Club Plum*
"Unprepared" *Setu*
"Immigrant Song;" "Read Pretty" *Unlikely Stories*
"Fuck Florida" Issue,
Variation of "Emerging Immigrant's Accents: This is the Spoken Birthright of
Bicultural Spanglish," *Autoethnography*
"What I Grapple With," "White Listening Subject," "Intersection," "Decisions,"
Rigorous

Publisher: Leah Huete de Maines
Editor: Christen Kincaid
Cover Art: Samuel Aldape
Author Photo: Daniel Reynolds
Cover Design: Elizabeth Maines McCleavy

Order online: www.finishinglinepress.com
also available on amazon.com

Author inquiries and mail orders:
Finishing Line Press
PO Box 1626
Georgetown, Kentucky 40324
USA

Contents

Spanglish..1

White Brown 4

Things I Can Say in My Mother's Language...5

What I Grapple With 6

Read Pretty 7

White Listening Subject..9

Decisions 10

America, America 11

Unprepared..13

Intersection 14

What Peruvians Do 15

Un día..16

Online Dating 17

Love and Language...18

La Comida de Peru...19

Wikipedia 20

Immigration Memoirs 22

The reason… 23

Immigrant Song...24

What Mother Says 25

White Latinas...26

The Clash of Century 27

What Good Peruvians Do 29

The Beat of my Heart 31

So You Don't Leave with the Wrong Idea...32

For my parents, Mercedes and Robert, who raised me so loved and supported to become a strong, independent American Latina.
For my older sister, Nicole, my guide and mentor, especially as a bicultural Latina.
For my abuelos, Maruja and Pepe, for leaving everything they knew to give me the opportunities I have today.
For all of those who have lived on the edge of multiple existences, especially mis primos y mis tios, for our white-brown experience.

Para mi padres, Mercedes y Robert, que me criaron tan amada y apoyada para convertirme en una latina estadounidense fuerte e independiente.
Para mi hermana mayor, Nicole, mi guía y mi mentora especialmente como es una latina bicultural.
Para mis abuelos, Maruja and Pepe, por dejar todo lo que sabían para darme las oportunidades que hoy tengo.
Para todos aquellos que han vivido al borde de múltiples existencias, especialmente mis primos y mis tíos, por nuestra existencia blanco-marrón.

Spanglish

Abuela's understanding of language changed when she came to the United States. From solely Spanish to a whole new classification of words and extension of herself. She asked strangers for directions when she barely knew "right" from "left." Her tongue developed accents. Peruvian ponchos, dark skin, and "broken" words—all looked upon through the calculated eyes of the white strangers.

Her home was for Spanish. Her new relatives talked it fluently. Mi mama learned the flip of the hand, the tip of the tongue, the wisp of their lilt. Her Spanish was—different. Words came easily—spelling, reading, writing was missing. Would likely be the only test she would fail. Whether semilingual or a "long time English language learner," both meaning not entirely proficient in two languages. She can edit and transpose in English yet says "pink shades" instead of "rose colored glasses." Blames her immigrant upbringing as quickly as her tongue rolls out native Spanish.

My tongue flips Spanish as a new-born babe flips to their stomach. Slowly, fruitlessly, filled with effort and attrition. I learned phrases but resisted my mother's attempts to give me her language. When I realized its importance time had flowed past the age of native and into the land of foreign and accents. When I learned in school I would ask for my mother's assistance, but I learned visually. I would ask for spellings and she would flounder. Fail the test. Create something unrecognizable, adaptive, wrong. She shrugged her shoulders at questions on conjugations.

"I don't know why, but I know that's right." She told me.

My Spanish floundered, fluctuated, eroded, but this I understood. Spanish was the whisper in my ear, that distant hum on the wind, the itch on the back of my skull. I grew upon it's wings even if I could not name the bird I flew on. There were some things I knew without having to be explained. "Por" and "Para," for one. Students questioned my methods and I shrugged at questions on rules.

"I don't know why, but I know that's right."

My lack of Spanish created a hole in my identity once I became an adult. My cousins in Peru could barely talk. My Spanish was punctured and venal— their English shattered and loose. Words slipped between us across google translate and dictionaries with cracked bindings. My vieja at nearly 100, whose memory eroded worse than my Spanish, recounted tales that my tio would need to translate. My name and parentage became a homage retold minutes apart as she delightfully inquired upon who I was.

My lack of Spanish led to the judgement.

A boy I dated, told me: "Anyone who doesn't know their family's home language should be ashamed of themselves."

I wish I had told him that not all of us were so privileged to be sent home to China for six months every year when they were children. How he shouldn't judge others just because they are not up to his standard. Instead, it became a mark across my chest that I tried to hide beneath thin clothing. I felt the pressure of not knowing my mother's native language.

"I'm Peruvian."

"So you speak Spanish?"

Gail Shuck (2006) discusses how "The relationship between talk about language and talk about race is not coincidental, nor are the similarities in those discourses superficial" (p. 260). Those whose English is corrupted and learning are looked down upon for not being of the predominant race. Similarly, in reverse, I am designed as solely the dominant race because my tongue is coated with "has been" and "because." Because I grapple with the words necessary to speak to my abuela in her native tongue, my Peruvian blood dries upon the still and is washed away with soap.

As a professor I wonder upon the day I teach students Latin American literature when their blood sings Spanish and their tongues rolls r's easier than it turns pudding. Years of study and knowledge cannot cover the breaks in my accent and the *gringa* in my phrasing. My birth name is White, my skin tone is White, my language is White. Motha (2014) says that "a definition of Whiteness is elusive because it is first and foremost understood in terms of what it is not, that is, a category of racial identity that is 'not racial minority' or 'not person of color'" (38). Being seen as white, my bicultural existence is erased along the page, leaving no imprint by which to recognize it had been there at all.

I have felt the weight of family that lives continents away. I have felt the weight of being an immigrant's daughter. I have felt the weight of being torn between two worlds. If I were to tell you about the language of my tongue it would be heavily accented and trilingual—Spanish, English, and everything that exists in between. My dream is to one day be able to bounce between Spanish and

English effortlessly and when I am angry—to do so to my children, who will understand me. I keep putting off this dream for others—pursuing a doctorate, raising a puppy, moving across the country multiple times—but that does not mean it does not exist. That does not mean I don't feel the weight of all those languages pressing on the back of my skull when hopeful eyes stare into mine and I can only gaze back in uncertainty. I am traveling soon to my cousins wedding in Ecuador, for she has married a man more Latino than anyone in our generation of familia, and I wonder how much I will be able to converse with the relatives I will meet there. I wait in terror at the thought of them being disappointed and talking behind my back about how I should know my abuela's language. How I should know what "Te amo" means not because I have learned it, but because I was raised to know it.

I wish I had not fought my mother so much. But now I will have to learn the hard way, and only hope that my children will allow me to teach them. So that one day they will not know what it means to not be fluent.

To not be fluent is to cock my head whenever I recognize Spanish, in both understanding and confusion. To not be fluent is to have Spanish speakers come up to me hopeful, only for me to turn them away. To not be fluent is to question what exists between my head, my tongue, and my pulse and where the words that flow out of me should actually go.

To not be fluent is to have an ache in my gut.

I wonder if it exists this way for my abuela, just with English instead.

White Brown

"You're Mediterranean, right?"

The words of strangers thrust against me as a cacophony of screamos with no melody. If I could wear my identity on my sleeve, I wonder what color it would take. Is there a way to summarize my skin tone through sighs?

"You're obviously Brazilian by the way you dance."

I thought about getting a tattoo of a Nazca line. A slightly more subtle way to paint Peru into my bones and smear the blood across my face. I wonder if I would stop being asked where I belonged on the globe as though I could spin it till I found my mark and point to it with only one finger. The new guy I'm seeing asked me what Nazca lines are.

"MEXICO! MEXICO!"

Peruvian. Polish. Irish. Italian. Chinese. Could my hand span the distances to pinpoint each part of the lands I was born with? My vieja denies having a Chinese grandmother. My abuela was teethed on thimbles filled with wine by her Italian father. Mi mama sung Selena as she cleaned. My grandmother on my other side still makes potato pancakes. My father is built on patriarchy and we both hide our emotions in bottles under our sleeves. What about the countries I've picked up along the way? Korea. Brazil. Ghana. How could I ink these lines into my skin to become one and nothing at the same time?

"You're very ethnically ambiguous."

As though I'm supposed to understand what that means.

Things I Can Say in My Mother's Language

Hello	Hola
My name is	Mi llamo es/Mi nombre es
Where is	Donde esta…?
I am 26	Tengo vente y sies anos
I'm from Michigan	Soy de Michigan
My mom is from Peru	Mi madre es de Peru
I have pain	Tengo me duele
I have tried to kill myself	
I have brown eyes	Tengo ojos café
I can sing	Puedo cantar
I feel dead inside	
I can't speak Spanish	No puedo hablar espanol
I should	Yo deberia
But I can't	Pero no puedo
I live in the US	Yo vivo en los Estado Unidos
I have been hospitalized 11 times	
Sometimes I can't breathe	A veces no puedo respirar
Sometimes I can't feel	A veces no puedo sentir
Sometimes I wish I were dead	

I don't have the words

What I Grapple With

I was born ambiguous, half of me would've been erased in the white plague. I cannot roll my r's and I hold little fear of police still I look more like princess Mia in the before picture than the beautiful one. I pronounce *llama* with a y and the only clothes that fit upon first try were found in Spain. I own three basic white girl chokers and my recent grown love for Starbucks sits heavy in my gut. I will never try pumpkin spice. No one wins a free drink on the guess my ethnicity game, even when given two truths and a lie. I sneezed for 24 hours the second time I went to my mother's home country, the first time I nearly died. If you threw light at me only my face would glow, still I would be seen. I write this wearing a Peruvian scarf sitting next to my rich white person's dog. If I were to be broken in pieces different countries would claim the biggest parts of me and what remained would dissipate into the confusion that is my white girl birth name with my brown girl nickname. Both feel distant when thrown in a random direction across the room. My sexuality bent. My interests bent. My name bent. If my gender were to become fluid I would disappear into a large lake one day while crossing. There is still time for that I guess.

What does whiteness mean to me NOW? What has it meant to me EVER?

Read Pretty

"Yet Smitherman's encounters show that even whites, supposedly the majority of non-dialect speakers, don't communicate in the accepted standard [English]."
-Young, 2009, 68

My white is caught on my throat
if I am not speaking English and my

Spanish is scrambled in the back of my

tongue decaying along with my

screams

then what am I actually saying?

My skin wears White my

hair wears Peru but

every-   one

tells me that my accent
does not bleed through.

I am aware I am

conquering

because my face does not match my blood

that not-English is what exists
on my tongue.

My abuelita speaks

broken

Spanish drips from the side of her -itos

all that she did
all she went through
so I could speak in
a language that she

understands

un poquito.

I am supposed to

teach

the not-English

the not-Spanish

code switching
saying their translingualism is lesser
than my

7

outdated/harmful/conquering/damagaging/genocidal/imperial/colonial
racism.

My Whiteness is caught in my throat
as I stand up here in front of
you
attempting to tell
that I am

trying

but I don't know what to do.

White Listening Subject

"to understand language is to understand how it gets linked to people. And I'm not talking about real people, but ideas about people" (Reyes 312)

I am Latina   You are Mexican
I am a female   You are small
I am Peruvian   You are bilingual
I am mentally ill   You are on drugs
I am skinny   You are healthy
I am sick   You are dying
I am Latina   You are hot blooded
I am female   You like men
I am Peruvian   You are short
I am mentally ill   You are unstable
I am skinny   You are not strong
I am sick   You are dying
I am Latina   You are traditional
I am female   You are a mom
I am Peruvian   You are dark skinned
I am mentally ill   You are pathetic
I am skinny   You are attractive
I am sick   You are dying
I am Latina   You are Mexican
I am a female   You are weak
I am Peruvian   You are bilingual
I am mentally ill   You are weak
I am skinny   You are healthy
I am sick   You are dying
I am Latina   You are weak
I am a female   You are weak
I am Peruvian   You are weak
I am mentally ill   You are weak
I am skinny   You are weak
I am sick   You are dying

Decisions

I listen to my Latin Dance playlist on Spotify attempting to pick the best song for my intro to creative writing class, through a Latin Literature lens, should listen to first. *Suavemente by Elvis Crespo? Do I want to start them with a classic or one they may recognize?* I plan out the opening conversation I will have to use to explain to them why we are studying and learning about Latin culture—why it matters to them and their discovery of identity. *Pepas by Farruko? It's a modern one—was played at my cousins Ecuadorian wedding— but there's no Latin radio station here.* I can picture the questioning, the resistance, as they fight not to learn about everything that makes me—me. *Propuesta Indecente by Romeo Santos? Do I really wanna start them with a bachata?!* Although I go through my roster and do not notice any Spanish last names, I still wonder if there will be students in this class more Hispanic than me. *Si Una Vez by Selena? Talk about classic, this would never be played in a club now a days.* Ones that will laugh and point at my poor pronunciation and lack of understanding of the Spanish language. *Shape of you Salsa Remix? But do I want to start them out with an ENGLISH salsa? They don't know the difference!* I remind myself of the family gatherings we had for years. *Danza Kuduro by Don Omar? They'd definitely know that but isn't that Portuguese not Spanish? Do I really wanna go down that rabbit hole?* I remind myself that I know how to dance the way they did in the clubs in Peru even though I was not born there. *The Macarena!* Despite the fact that I cannot roll my r's. *Oh GOD no.* I wonder how my white students will struggle with the steps to bachata. *Which cuts anything by Prince Royce...* I wonder how on earth I can find a partner to help me demonstrate the moves to them in a white, republican town called Normal. *Didn't Ricky Martin just have a scandal?!?* I wonder at what critique they will leave for me at the end of class, if they will have hated every Latina moment I showed them.

Vivir mi Vida the version by Cherito may be my best bet...

I have to pick the right song.

It starts in French?!

America, America

"America had defined and would continue to define itself most successfully by what it rejected, not by what it was." (Dolmage 52)[1]

O say! can you see—Ngai[2] discusses how when first creating immigrant laws, the US allowed a certain amount of people in the country based off the people who already lived in the country of the same nationality.

by the dawns early light—"the board defined "native stock," not as persons born in the United States, but as persons who descended from the white population of the United States in 1790. It defined "foreign stock" as the descendants of all whites who immigrated to the United States after 1790. (72)

what so proudly we hailed—"The law stipulated that "inhabitants in continental United States in 1920' does not include (1) immigrants from the [Western Hemisphere] or their descendants, (2) aliens ineligible to citizenship or their descendants, (3) the descendants of slave immigrants, or (4) the descendants of the American aborigines." (72)

at the twilights last gleaming—"It subtracted from the total United States population all blacks and mulattoes, eliding the difference between the "descendants of slave immigrants" and the descendants of free Negroes and voluntary immigrants from Africa." (72)

whose broad stripes and bright stars—"the law excised all nonwhite, non-European peoples from that vision, erasing them from the American nationality." (72)

through the perilous fight—while the immigration quota for white nations existed between 1,304 for Belgium to 65,721 from Great Britain and Northern Ireland, minority countries maxed out at only 100 people allowed in the year annually beginning July 1st 1929. (74)

o'er the ramparts we watched—"In a sense, demographic data were to twentieth-century racists what craniometric data had been to race scientists during the nineteenth." (77)

---

[1] Dolmage, Jay. "Disabled Upon Arrival: The Rhetorical Construction of Disability and Race at Ellis Island." *Cultural Critique*, vol. 77, 2011, pp. 24-69.
[2] Ngai, Mae M. "The Architecture of Race in American Immigration Law: A Reexamination of the Immigration Act of 1924." *The Journal of American History, vol. 86, no. 1, 1999, pp. 67–92, https://doi.org/10.2307/2567407.*

were so gallantly streaming—"If statistics showed that immigrants were less healthy, less educated, and poorer than native-born Americans, that was deemed evidence of the immigrants' inferior physical constitution, intelligence, and ambition." (77)

and the rocket's red glare—"The Quota Board also ignored intermarriage between Euro-Americans and both African Americans and Native American Indians, never problematizing the effect of miscegenation on the "origins" of the white population." (79)

the bombs bursting in air—"A more honest inquiry might have concluded that determining the national origins of the American people was theoretically suspect and methodologically impossible" (80)

gave proof through the night—"The system of quotas based on national origin was the first major pillar of the Immigration Act of 1924. The second was the exclusion of persons ineligible to citizenship. By one account, the provision barred half of the world's population from entering the United States." (80)

that our flag was still there—"Ineligibility to citizenship and exclusion applied to the peoples of all the nations of the far east." (80)

o say! does that star-spangled—"Nearly all Asians had already been excluded, either by the Chinese exclusion laws or by the "barred Asiatic zone" the Congress created in 1917." (80)

banner yet wave—"The Nationality Act of 1870 thus encoded racial prerequisities to citizenship according to the familiar classifications of black and white." (81)

O'er the land of the free—"the federal courts' ruling in naturalization cases increasingly rejected scientific explanations in favor of common understandings of race." (81)

and the home of the—"The Immigration Act of 1924 contributed to the racialization of immigrant groups around notions of whiteness, permanent foreignness, and illegality—categories of differences that have outlived the racial categories created by eugenics and post-World War I nativism." (92)

brave—"Those legacies remain with us to this day... in 'racial formations that are the material trace of history.'" (92)

Unprepared

I desire to debate white privilege when I am benefiting from its clutch. I desire to debate my racial heritage in a classroom with students who are more Latina than I am. Facing them, mouth open, mind alert, I draw a blank as to what can capture the problem. Where one of my African American students writes a memoir about being shot in the eye while one of my white students writes about football. My African American students call African American vernacular "slang" and none of them know what code switching is but do it naturally. I am aware I am meant to mentor their racial awareness but when one of my students starts trapped for five weeks in China while another grew up in rural Aurora, the starting points are in separate oceans. Neither one of them answers my questions about positionality, nor answer when I ask what they call a highway. Pulling teeth for easy answers means silence for ones on racial theory, in the end I am the one left toothless without the ability to say *the problem* anymore.

Intersection

"Adrienne Rich argues that we cannot separate race, class, and sex oppression, since they are 'experienced simultaneously.'" (Inoue 374)

Brown
                    Female
                                        Middle Class
Latin
                    Girl
                              Food stamps
          Curly
                    Woman
                                   Steady income
               Short
                    Vagina
                         Health insurance
                    Colored
                    Lady
                    No dental or vision
          Unpaid [summers] tan
                    Maiden
                                   Peruvian
          Parental support
                    Damsel
                                        Hispanic
          Skipping meals
                    Senorita
                                        Spanish [said in English]
Minority Scholarships

What Peruvians Do

Put avocado and aji on EVERYTHING. Potatoes, meats, vegetables, socks, you name it. Drink you under the table. Not with your flimsy US beer either, but with REAL beer, with a percentage that's meant to knock you sideways. Know not to talk back to your mama or she'll smack you across the room. Or your papa, or your tia, or your abuela, or your tio, or your abuelo, or that stranger whose older than you. Just if it sounds sassy assume you shouldn't say it to them. We do talk with sass though, most of the time. WE NEVER YELL WE JUST TALK LOUDLY. We talk to three people—*si mama estoy comiendo*—about different things—*MIJO LEVANTANSE AHORA*—all in— *que linda, preciosa*—the same breath. We sing loudly and sometimes on key. The same could be said with dancing—loudly and sometimes on key. We don't leave, the house just gets bigger. *Familia* is a term applied generously and you have to give everyone who falls under that category a hug and kiss every time you enter or leave a room—*in the time it takes you to talk back to me you could've done it already.* We wear red and white for spirit and play an instrumental national anthem that competes against your five tias who don't HAVE to sing louder than it but most definitely will. There is no privacy, no semblance of boundaries, no space to be found—introverts beware.

But when they're gone, you feel it. Alone, across the country, you feel it.

"monolingual habitus, the assumption that use of a language other than English must signal an inability to use English, as though no one in their right mind would voluntarily choose to use any other language." (Motha, 2014, 51)

Un día

Tomando medidas para escupir en las voluminosas secuelas de cuatro voces gritando en la esquina de ese documento de Word desde las habitaciones que han tallado en mi cuerpo. Poder decir algo sobre las manzanas con palabras reales detrás del brillo rojo aplastando bajo la espera de lo que no puedo olvidar que fueron utilizadas. Olvidando recordar olvidar la presión entre mis piernas, de semen/sangre fluyendo por el vértice de mi no. Sosteniendo algo ... siendo sostenido sin que sus palabras me envolvieran la garganta para cortarme a mitad de la canción. Mirando hacia arriba en lugar de a través del goteo a lo largo de la esquina de mis brazos a medida que se disuelven, extendidos. Finalmente, tal vez, si: liberado con un zumbido mientras mi espalda almidonada respira en tu mano abierta.

Online Dating

We swap playlists and attitude while summarizing our complex heritage into one word differentiated by the gender marker at the end of it. When I think of the past men in my life who were all important to me, they were all—white—like my father and me their faces turned red in the sun as they spun falsehoods as intricate and deep as the scissor marks across my stomach. I wonder if it is different because we share a noun, I wonder if it is different at all. I tell you I am trusting and can't understand your sarcasm, you use it less in the following conversation. I wanted to marry a man who could make my children more Hispanic than me. I forget the other matches and let the likes pile up but wonder if it is different. How is it different? The men who raped me burned in the sun. The best man I know does the same. Is it because they are from the US, it is because they were not raised with Latina madres who beat sensibility into them, is it because they would not recognize *Suavemente* against *La Copa de La Vida*? Would you never rape me because you are Latino or because you are you? Is being afraid of white men a hypothesis that has been proven or a stereotype that has done the same? My face and shoulders burn in the sun the same way all of them did. I am half white. The children I bear will be part white. Will I fear the son that I raise?

'Course you ghost me in the end so did you even prove Latinos are any different?

Love and Language

We met at five (or at least we could have). You carried your
sister (who was a spider) on your back
while I wore that sweater (someone else gave me).
       Probé (pruebo) decir tu nombre
       pero mi lengua esta atrapada entre
       tu mano y la araña y la idioma
         mi madre que no sé.
Pero it slips entre the floorboards dónde
tu hermanas sleeps beside la luna and
the timer.

La Comida de Peru

El tipos de papa y pesca couldn't be contained in a large community. Yet my tongue has only tasted enough to be taken in two hands cupped together. My favorite as a child: nothing. My favorite as an adult: tsukemen first, *aji de gallina* second. Mi abuelo would laugh in his burial place when I applied chopsticks. My tongue ventured continents across Los Angeles and returned to Asian cuisine. Mi mama made me *tallarines verdes con filete* and I vomited in the kitchen sink. If my stomach could agree with my heart, it would bleed *huancaina* and be soaped up on papa. Yet with the nearest Aji two and half hours away, I suck down sushi AYCE as the usual.

Wikipedia

"Peruvians are expressive, using hand gestures when talking and are tactile, expecting a kiss on the cheek for hi and bye."

Wikipedia labels—me, my family,
my mother's homeland—in
small sounds: "tactile."
years of history, tradition—
words without context.

I remember the expanse of
lips on my face.
Men shook hands.
Everyone kissed *me*.
Bursts akin to
rose petals made of
fire.

My vieja asking me
who I was.
My cousins of various ages.
The boys in Capoeira who
I had never met.
Petals, warming my face.

Family, strangers, everyone
kissed me.

I cried when I left.

Distant waves, handshakes,
hugs seldom, kisses
nonexistent.
Holes encroaching—
an empty flower bed.

Peruvians dealing with Covid.
Will kissing strangers
simply cease to exist?

The only place I
felt truly welcomed
embraced
touched
just... gone?

My face feels cold.
Are we still
"tactile"?

Immigration Memoirs

18th and 19th century. The white immigrants to the Americas or London float with luggage carried by their single servant. *How will I survive having to do work myself?* An ambassador is: recommended an Arabic poem, pesters her translators, rebuffs their work, transcribes it into English phrasing. *How improved.* The white ones wrap themselves in blue jewels and colored sweat, prostate their English as though anything else is offensive—the black ones fear for their lives. There is no mention of Latin ones. I study them against modern day memoirs. Stories of women wrapped in worms and starvation in their home country, abused by patriarchy on their ponytail in the US. Refugees who yearn for safety and sanity to be dismissed for colored degrees, education a rigged system and their only option. No welfare/healthcare/jobs. US thrives on backs in grease.

The reason…

… I am so desperate is my tongue
hangs like lead without tools
to lift it into my skull

… he is so curious is he turns
to bachata but doesn't
understand the stanzas.

… she knows is her familia
raised her to transpose
the borders with her words.

… he studies is his father
did ahead of him, made a wage
with another's language.

… I want is the lilt in my
laugh isolates me as
a gringa (a white insult),
a badge I wear with shame.

… he endured is for the resume.
he desires is to dart around
land whose people his country denied.

… Por mi familia, mi abuela—
my abuela's blood howls.
my abuela was birthed in this song.
my abuela knows no other.
my abuela had no option.

… While you people
pay $19.99 a month
to speak it with
a forked tongue
you people also
"speak English"

Immigrant Song

"To be an immigrant is to [always] be marked by the border." (Dolmage 27)

Hello my name is [Oh beautiful] I come from [for spacious skies] I am running from [for amber waves] if they catch me they will [of grain] and no one survives that.

Hello my name is [for purple mountains] I just turned THIS many. My mother is in [majesties] my father is dead. My brothers and I came [above the] and hopefully one day I'll become a [fruited plains].

Hello my name is [America]. I come from [America]. I helped you and [God shed his grace]. Please [on thee] want to [and crown thy good] they will [with brotherhood]. Please [from sea] help [to shining] please [sea].

What Mother Says

The difference of a couple decades
plays out in waves
across our breaths.

My mother needs confirmation she will
never end up in a nursing home.
A mumbled yes she has heard
across the decades will
not suffice
to eat away the anxiety.

The stories flit through her trauma
like bricks through a window.
Shattering like raindrops,
sharp edge on naked flesh.
Deep down I think
she worries about her Americanized
daughters. She rarely calls us *hijas*.

She laments how her illness prevents her
from caring por su mama,
how she is left to the eldest hija.
When asked, she will say United
Statians are more open than
her elderly catholic, Latino padres.
Her primos in Peru could
not hear her troubles.

I told my mom the first time
I had sex
I never worried about reprimand.
Mis primos were
nowhere to be seen.
So I call my mother daily.
My USian friends said all of it
was weird. I wonder
if my mother is correct.

I've always wondered
how United Statian mothers
reprimand their daughters.

White Latinas

My sister reaffirms we are "white Latinas." As children in white communities, we felt the darkness of our skin as a badge of honor, difference, exception. The "otherness" was a specialness that crept up the back of our spines to hold our shoulders in place and keep our chins up. In accepting communities, sharing alfajores meant the powdered sugar frosting lips like a love language. Knowing details about Peru meant your team won the trivia prize, almost as useful as your reading of Norse mythology. To this day that happens sometimes.

As adults in Latin populated communities, the white of our skin burned out our tongues as we were "othered" for completely separate reasons. You realize you know more about Norse mythology than you do about your mother's native country. Returning to Peru for the first time since you were a baby (and nearly died) felt foreign—despite the fact their clothes hugged your curves in ways American stores left lacking, the ankles were all a bit short. You sneeze for twenty-four hours straight and wonder if you are being rejected by Peru itself. As you cocked your head for Spanish the laughter of tus amigas swooped over your head like a hawk on the hunt. My mother talks about the connections su prima was able to make with the familia by living in Peru until adulthood. This prima's English is accented. She is othered for reasons entirely different.

The Clash of the Century

is an issue of volume.
As a child I spoke out but
could never be heard above
the endless cascade of
mis tios, padres, abuelos.

Their voices hung on
the music in their own melody,
lulled the children to sleep
better than the rapture
of Latin drums.
All the more when
they spoke Spanish.

Their lullaby
disappears
in the bustle of the open air,
slurped up by the sounds
of a public who never
heard a cajón
played by hand.

The cries of their children
cut through more
than an immigrant
would ever dare.

As an adult I am constantly
reprimanded for speaking
too loudly, by mi familia.

Years of vocal training means
my voice is sharp,
carries across rooms
in successive beats
that disrupt the dull
of the passersby.

My therapist and I debate—
is my lack of control
a symptom of
my disease or
my trauma?

I wrap myself in the silence
of screaming punk music,
at ease that as an octave
lower my voice cannot
cut through.

My crying stopped
years ago, the tears turning
inwards and filling my belly
along with the pills.

I am unable to discuss
the volume of
when I am in trouble.

What Good Peruvians Do

The moment I was passed over
for a part in a play
the definition of a
wine bottle
changed for me.

I am Peruvian, so as was tradition
I tried wine, even though
I was only seventeen.
I had a little bit of the red stuff
ever since first communion—
I hated but drank anyways
because Peruvians were good Catholics.

Red wine will always taste
like church. White wine,
like adulthood,
familia.

When I was ten I had a sip of white,
made a face, spit it back.
The Peruvians picked on me,
told me:
you will love it,
wine/alcohol/beer
you will drink everyone
under the table.
Because that's what Peruvians do.

I don't know what kind of wine
had been in that bottle before
I broke it.

The anger came from many traumatic things
I wouldn't have the words for until years later.

The family we had in Peru
never moved out. Lived within
ten minutes walking from each other.
Primos, tios, abuelos—
saw each other every day.

But now it was not wine.

The Peruvian family
we had in the United States
split and scattered.
I saw them once a year
if I was lucky.
My hermana, primos, tios,
all miles away.

It was glass.

I was a good Peruvian.

Broken glass.

I had no one to tell.

Glass that I drew
across my arm
until I bled.

The Beat of my Heart

My Ghanaian drum teacher talks about how babies are carried on the backs of their mothers to the beat of the drum song. If mi familia were to encapsulate the beat of our breaths into one rhythm it would be salsa. Mis primos and I didn't realize it until I started taking Latin dance lessons. Huayno and marinera hum through my skin as a hammer which vibrates my blood and caught my feet in a befuddled net. Sensual bachata is a romance between swans whose necks can't be controlled by bones. Cumbia: a basic step that bumped to any rhythm as a familiar neighbor whose name you never learned yet homemade spicy salsa tastes like a comfortable cream on the tip of your tongue. But the eight beat, six step dance accompanied by the drums our abuelas never taught us to play brought us to tears as adults.

My abuelo was the keeper of the records. He *was* the music and brought it to all our gatherings. My grand tio talks about how he siempre danced with mi abuela porque mi abuelo would be spinning his records, playing his drums, singing. I was six when he passed—my memoires isolated to his half smile and the tube in his mouth. When the grand tios aged and our group fell apart, I dreamed in a salsa that would call them home from hitch hiking rides to a doctor's office they no longer worked at. My future is marked by a record player and a Spotify playlist, even as the salsa I dream in crumbles beneath the pressure of my chest swaying to the beat of a bachata. When I tried to teach my abuela, I discovered how strongly she could resist. The salsa of Callao, her hometown, was in her aged feet enough that she did not need her cane to keep her afloat. As I grow and am called by swing or waltz, the salsa rests in my chest as a wide stone nestled in a small palm. All encompassing and unchanging.

So You Don't Leave with the Wrong Idea

I wanted to end on a note of joy.
My poems are filled with
questions/pain/complexity/disappointment
Writing is a form of
healing. Writing is a form of
trauma. Bicultural living
is the same.

The meaning to
Amor Prohibido by Selena
eludes me. But I belt her high notes
to remember my mother's
hip movement, as cleaners filled the air.
I am five and have no nightmares.
I cry for other reasons.

A Peruvian flag
flaps on my balcony,
fades in sun,
marks my apartment
for all my friends.

I stumble over my Spanish,
asking *Como se dice...*
more times than I
am confident.
Yet my abuela delights
every time I tell her
I'm graduating
una programa de doctora.
No, no medico doctora jaja.

Bachata rolls through
my spine with the ease
water runs down an icicle.
I teach it to my boyfriend
on the carpet of our home.
My fondest memory
is throwing up my hands
No pares (sigue! sigue!)
surrounded by familia

whose names I forget but
who love me. Remark
how beautiful I've grown
as they ask me questions
my white family never does.

It's hard to end on a happy note.
When many things change:
my familia's locations,
my Spanish gravitating/abating,
my relationship to my mother
and her patria. But some things
never do.

Cuando mi prima y mi hermana
married men in separate
states and countries in
the same year. Many people
cancelled, dropped, pulled, filled with
excuses/apologies/empty words,
the Castro clan (la nombre de
la familia de mi mama)
always came through.

Kayla Williams (as she is first and foremost known) was raised in Michigan and didn't learn that fudge could come from places OTHER than Mackinac Island until much too late. Her mother was born in Peru, while her father is many generations removed Polish She thanks her English teacher Andrew Wood for encouraging her to get her undergraduate degree in writing from Grand Valley State University where she started to train Capoeira, an Afro-Brazilian martial arts, and picked up the nickname "Pica Pau" or "Pica" as she tends to go by more commonly now. Some honorable mentions from this time: Todd Kaneko, who taught her she could be a creative writer, Amorak Huey, who taught her poetry could be fun, and Chris Haven who mentored her through her McNair program and enabled her to go enter grad school.

She was able to get into her first-choice master's program at California Institute of Arts where she was turned from a fiction writer to a nonfiction writer who also explores poetry and hybrid form. She came out as an experimental writer and has not been able to stop playing with form ever since. Some honorable mentions from this time: Gabrielle Civil, who taught her nonfiction was her art and experimental style was incredible, Douglas Kearney, who brought her poetry from a musing to an understanding, and Brian Evenson, who mentored her for two whole years with enthusiasm and still offers her support now.

During the pandemic she started at Illinois State University, where her current work with chair Ela Przybylo is some of the nonfiction writing she is most proud of. She is currently working on many different projects: her dissertation, an experimental nonfiction essay collection on the ways the US health care is biased and inaccessible; a poetry chapbook about racial themes and issues; a magical realism piece about growing up an immigrant's daughter in a world where immigrants receive physical bruises from being outcasted; and fantasy love story about a young prince and his powerful, stoic female guard. She like many writers is guilty of too many stories in her head and not enough hands to type them out.

She thanks you all for your continued support by reading her book, and especially thanks those who actually read the extent of this bio. Normally she would say "happy reading" but this book is not entirely happy so she will simply say "thanks again." Find her @KaylaPicaWilliams.bsky.social